What's News in Zoos?

Pamela Rushby

What's News in Zoos?

Text: Pamela Rushby
Publishers: Tania Mazzeo and Eliza Webb
Series consultant: Amanda Sutera
　Hands on Heads Consulting
Editor: Laken Ballinger
Project editor: Annabel Smith
Designer: Leigh Ashforth
Project designer: Danielle Maccarone
Illustrations: Wayne Murphy
Permissions researcher: Liz McShane
Production controller: Renee Tome

Acknowledgements
We would like to thank the following for permission to reproduce copyright material:

Front cover, pp. 4, 22: iStock.com/ajr_images; pp. 1, 5 (bottom right), 19, 23, back cover: iStock.com/Henk Hulshof; pp. 3, 14: EyeEm/Kiran Chourasia; pp. 5 (top left), 6: Dreamstime.com/Hannator92; pp. 5 (top right), 11: Media Bakery/Dave Stamboulis; pp. 5 (bottom left), 15: Getty Images/Anadolu Agency; p. 7: Alamy Stock Photo/Tatyana Tomsickova; p. 8 (top): Alamy Stock Photo/Maurice Savage, (bottom): Alamy Stock Photo/Bill Bachman; p. 9: iStock.com/elmvilla; p. 10: Shutterstock.com/Mike Workman; p. 12: iStock.com/barbaraaaa; p. 13 (top): iStock.com/Tochukwu Ngene, (bottom): Shutterstock.com/Sebastian22; pp. 16, 17: Getty Images/BIJU BORO; p. 18: Shutterstock.com/Maridav; p. 20: Alamy Stock Photo/GH Photos; p. 21: Getty Images/Mel Melcon.

Every effort has been made to trace and acknowledge copyright. However, if any infringement has occurred, the publishers tender their apologies and invite the copyright holders to contact them.

NovaStar

Text © 2024 Cengage Learning Australia Pty Limited

ISBN 978 0 17 033391 7

Cengage Learning Australia
Level 5, 80 Dorcas Street
Southbank VIC 3006 Australia
Phone: 1300 790 853
Email: aust.nelsonprimary@cengage.com

For learning solutions, visit **cengage.com.au**

Printed in Australia by Ligare Pty Limited
1 2 3 4 5 6 7 28 27 26 25 24

Nelson acknowledges the Traditional Owners and Custodians of the lands of all First Nations Peoples. We pay respect to Elders past and present, and extend that respect to all First Nations Peoples today.

Contents

Welcome! — 4

Different Kinds of Zoos — 6

Saving Tree Kangaroos — 10

Black Softshell Turtle Numbers Grow — 14

California Condors Fly Free Again! — 18

Keep Visiting Zoos! — 22

Glossary — 23

Index — 24

Welcome!

Hi, I'm Zac! You've found my vlog – or video blog – *What's News in Zoos?* I work as a keeper, or someone who takes care of animals, in a big city zoo.

A zoo is a place where animals are kept and looked after. Zoos are also where important work in animal research, education and **conservation** is carried out. They are places where people can see animals that they might not get to see anywhere else.

I have friends all over the world who work in zoos. Here on my vlog, you can watch the videos they send me. You can also watch my own video about some of the different kinds of zoos.

Different Kinds of Zoos

Saving Tree Kangaroos

Black Softshell Turtle
Numbers Grow

California Condors
Fly Free Again!

Different Kinds of Zoos

Animals live in **enclosures** in most zoos, such as the Taronga Zoo in Sydney, Australia, the Auckland Zoo in Aotearoa New Zealand and the London Zoo in England. Enclosures keep animals safely in an area. They have plants and water to make them feel like the animals' **habitats** in the wild.

Zoo enclosures let visitors see the animals safely, in a place that feels like the animals' habitat.

Petting zoos have animals that usually live on farms or are kept as pets, such as rabbits, goats and chickens. Animals in these types of zoos are used to being around people, so visitors can stroke and cuddle them. Petting zoos can also be found in larger zoos and parks.

Visitors can get close to different animals in a petting zoo.

Open-range zoos have plenty of space for animals to walk around. The San Diego Zoo in the USA has an animal park with a very large open area.

Giraffes walk together through a large space in the San Diego Zoo.

Most open-range zoos are also **safari parks**. At safari parks, visitors are driven around in special vehicles to see the wildlife, or visitors can drive through in their own cars. The Fuji Safari Park in Japan is even open at night, so visitors can see the **nocturnal** animals as well.

An ostrich comes close to visitors in a safari park bus at Werribee Zoo, an open-range zoo in Victoria, Australia.

There are even larger areas of land where animals can live freely and safely, called **game reserves**. Visitors can drive through the reserves to see if they can spot the animals. In Bandhavgarh (say: *Bund-uv-gar*) National Park in India, tigers can be seen in the wild.

A Bengal tiger walks down a road in the Bandhavgarh National Park.

Saving Tree Kangaroos

My friend Jacob sent this video about zoos that work with a local community in Papua New Guinea to save the tree kangaroos.

Jacob in Papua New Guinea

Kangaroos that climb trees? These tree kangaroos found in Papua New Guinea do!

Tree kangaroos are **rare**, but they were becoming even rarer. They had begun disappearing because their natural habitat was being cleared for farming. People were also hunting the tree kangaroos for food.

Tree kangaroos in Papua New Guinea are rare in the wild.

The World Association of Zoos and **Aquariums** started a farming program with the local community. They began helping communities to grow new and different kinds of foods to try to stop tree kangaroos from being hunted. This has helped tree kangaroo numbers go up.

Tree kangaroos use their long tails to balance when they climb trees.

By growing new foods, communities in Papua New Guinea can help save the rainforest habitat.

Bananas can be farmed to help provide new food for communities in Papua New Guinea.

Black Softshell Turtle Numbers Grow

Pushpa lives in India and works in a zoo that helps to save **endangered** turtles. Here's her video!

Pushpa at her zoo in India

The black softshell turtle once lived in large numbers in **wetlands** and streams near the Brahmaputra (say: *Bra-ma-poo-tra*) River in India. However, over time, too many of these turtles were hunted for their meat and shells.

The black softshell turtle likes to live where there's lots of fresh water.

In 2002, the turtles were thought to be **extinct** in the wild. The only black softshell turtles that were left lived in **captivity** in a small, crowded pond on the grounds of a **temple**.

People gather at the temple pond in India where the last black softshell turtles were found.

Scientists in India worked to make the pond at the temple more comfortable for the turtles. This helped the turtles to **breed** and lay more eggs. In 2014, around 40 baby turtles hatched! They were moved to a special pond at the Assam State Zoo in India. When they were six months old, they were released into the wild. Since then, even more turtles have been raised and released.

A man who works at the temple to help care for the turtles checks some new eggs that have been laid.

California Condors Fly Free Again!

Daisy from the USA studies condors, which are very large birds. Click to watch her video!

Daisy in the desert in California

The California condor is one of the world's rarest birds. These condors once lived along the coast of the Pacific Ocean in California, USA. But when large numbers of people came to live in that area, the California condors began to disappear. This was because they were hunted and poisoned, and people stole their eggs to sell. By the early 1980s, there were only about 20 California condors left.

A California condor spreads its large wings.

It was decided that the only way to save the California condor would be through a **captive breeding program**. That meant the California condors would be looked after in zoos.

So, in 1987, the United States Fish and Wildlife Service teamed up with the Los Angeles Zoo and the San Diego Zoo Wildlife Alliance to begin the breeding program. All the California condors that were left in the wild were captured.

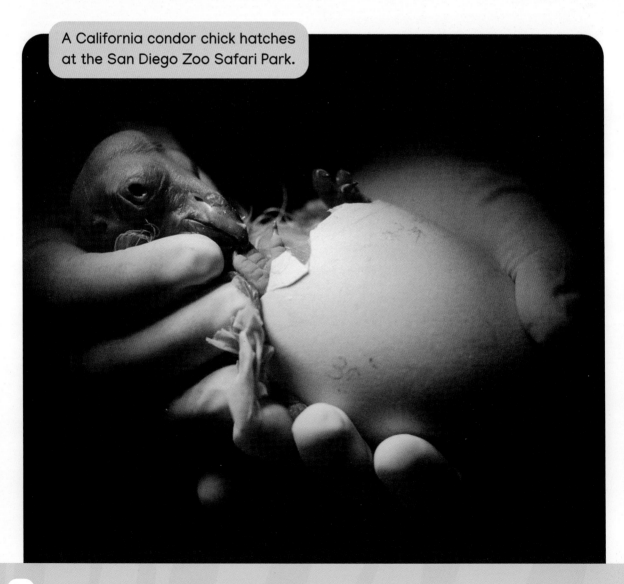

A California condor chick hatches at the San Diego Zoo Safari Park.

A California condor is released into the wild.

The program started to work, so some of the California condors were released back into the wild. Now, there are almost 500 California condors, with more than half of them living in the wild. They are protected by law, so no one is allowed to hurt them.

Keep Visiting Zoos!

Many people love to visit zoos. They can see and learn about rare animals and animals from places far away. Zoos are also where very important work is done, such as setting up conservation programs that help stop endangered animals from becoming extinct.

Keep checking my vlog! I'll be posting great news stories about the amazing work that's being done with the help of zoos all around the world.

Glossary

aquariums (*noun*) — buildings where sea life is kept and looked after

breed (*verb*) — to produce young

captive breeding program (*noun*) — when animals are kept in zoos so they can produce young

captivity (*noun*) — the keeping of animals in certain areas

conservation (*noun*) — protection of wildlife and the environment

enclosures (*noun*) — areas surrounded by a fence or a wall

endangered (*adjective*) — at risk of dying out

extinct (*adjective*) — when a type of animal is gone forever

game reserves (*noun*) — areas where native animals live free and are protected

habitats (*noun*) — places where animals usually live

nocturnal (*adjective*) — active at night

open-range zoos (*noun*) — very large enclosed areas where animals walk around freely

rare (*adjective*) — hardly ever found

safari parks (*noun*) — large zoos people drive through in vehicles to see animals

temple (*noun*) — a building for praying to gods

wetlands (*noun*) — land where there is a lot of water

Index

aquariums   12, 23

Bandhavgarh National Park   9

black softshell turtles   5, 14–17

California condors   5, 18–21

captive breeding program   20–21, 23

community   10, 12, 13

conservation   5, 22, 23

Fuji Safari Park   8

game reserves   9, 23

habitats   6, 11, 23

Los Angeles Zoo   20

open-range zoos   8, 23

petting zoos   7

safari parks   8, 23

San Diego Zoo   8, 20

tree kangaroos   5, 10–13

wetlands   15, 23